FBI
My Days Gone By

65 Years of Law Enforcement

JIM BRADY

WESTBOW
PRESS®
A DIVISION OF THOMAS NELSON
& ZONDERVAN

WestBow Press books may be ordered through booksellers or by contacting:

WestBow Press
A Division of Thomas Nelson & Zondervan
1663 Liberty Drive
Bloomington, IN 47403
www.westbowpress.com
844-714-3454

ISBN: 978-1-6642-5267-7 (sc)
ISBN: 978-1-6642-5269-1 (hc)
ISBN: 978-1-6642-5268-4 (e)

Library of Congress Control Number: 2021924903

Print information available on the last page.

WestBow Press rev. date: 06/15/2022

TABLE OF CONTENTS

PREFACE

I have considered publishing a book for many years from the encouragements of my wife, Verna, and many friends, some whom have known me all of my 33 years in the FBI, and 10 years as a Special Agent of State ABC.

I was also on the Governor's Task Force, four years as a Deputy Sheriff of Sumner County, Tennessee, three years of government security checks for Omniplex World Services Corporation. Finally, 15 years, as the owner of Investigative Services and Technologies, Inc.

This totals 65 years of some type of law enforcement and I think that is enough. It has been determined I am the oldest living retired employee if the Memphis division of the Bureau.

The reason for so many encouragements is that I remember, and was involved in, many historical cases in the division that no one would ever know about if it were not recorded in a book. I personally worked on these Memphis Div. cases from 1960 thru 1986 in some assignment.

I dedicate this book, first to God, for letting me live this life, to Verna, my lovely wife, my entire family, friends and to everyone who reads this book. *1* ESPECIALLY NOW THANKS, TO THE 59 DEDICATED EMPLOYEES

OF THE OFFICE FORCE, WHO WITHOUT THEM NO OFFICE COULD SURVIVE.

I hope you enjoy some of my stories from the Golden Years of the FBI.

Your Friend,
Jim Brady

ACKNOWLEDGEMENTS

Also Thanks to Gilbert and Myrna Wilks for their help in preparing this manuscript for publication.

I also appreciate the people at Westbow Press, a Division of Thomas Nelson, for their advice and cooperation.

I appreciate, very much, the comments made by my special friends who are recommending this book.

FOREWORD

by Hank Hillin

Writing a view lines for Jim Brady's book is a pleasure, not a task. You see, Jim Brady is one of my top five best and closest friends; and one of the finest and best persons I've ever known, a devout Christian Southern gentleman.

I have known Jim since 1962 when he met my plane at the Memphis airport, then drove me and two other FBI agents directly to Oxford Mississippi, to join a group of FBI employees assembling there to represent the Bureau's interest in a riot about to take place on the campus at the University of Mississippi. (Ole Miss.)

Our boss in that operation was Special Agent in charge Karl Dissly whose philosophy of leadership was, as he told me: assign the best people you have to do a job, and then get out of the way.

SAC Dissly had done that with having Jim Brady keep us all straight and on task that week of firearms being discharged, cars being burned, screaming and yelling student agitators breaking windows, all rioting.

Well, I saw the best at work that weekend in Jim Brady and he's been my friend and fellow FBI employee since.

Jim Brady has served a number of FBI bosses in every kind of case since then and he shows the same kind of care and concern in this book. I know you'll enjoy Jim's writing, which I think he is great at it and I know of no one better qualified or deserving.

Hank Hillin, FBI Agent
955--80
1981 elected Sheriff Nashville, Tn.
Past Army Intelligence Agent

To All Americans …
Thanks
and to my family:

My Lovely Wife, Verna of 65 Years
Two sons, Stan,(Deceased) and Steve,
Two Daughter-in-Laws
Six Grand Children
Four Great Grand Children

Special Thanks to Sandi
The best Daughter-in-law in the world
for taking most of the photos for this book.

The Mandrell Family
Father, Irby, Mother Mary,
Irlene, Barbara and Louise
My Law-Abiding Dad,
Bailiff of Corinth, Mississippi
Dad   and   Mom
"You Are Gone …
but your loving influence
will always be present."

Nashville, Music City
those good friends,
The Grand Ole Opry Family

Rush and Kate Brady

FOREWORD

by Rush Brady

In 1950, Corinth, Mississippi, was not a place anyone wanted to be, but some *had* to be there. James Brady had to be there! As a product of the Deep South, James Brady was raised in an inherently racist community. Fortunately, Mr. Brady was unique because of his morality and integrity. He tended to set himself apart from the truly uniform feeling of segregation. Perhaps it was his morality that drove him to protect and facilitate the Civil Right's Movement in the late 1950's and early 1960's via his position in the Federal Bureau of Investigation.

In order to understand the man who is James Brady, it helps to understand the circumstances in which he was raised. He was born in 1931, when the depression was at its bleakest. Nowhere were the hard times any harder than in the rural South. Mr. Brady would probably never say he was poor, and there were those who had less, but even the necessities were often luxurious ... and luxuries were something only those in the movies had.

Composed of a towering figure, that nonetheless is accompanied by a size thirteen shoe, this six-foot-three giant has a most-fitting sense of self. Like the proverbial gentle giant, Mr. Brady's size and stature hardly compare with the enormity of his experiences in comparison to the over-powering humility that he exudes. All included, somehow, he is the most welcoming and approachable man one may encounter. He takes his seat, aware of his size, fumbling with the awkwardly small swivel chair in his office. Embodying the very definition of Walter Mitty, James Brady's seemingly humdrum lifestyle is heavily shadowed by the incredible story-like adventures that he has both started and enjoyed. Humbly hanging on his walls are the countless awards and honors, but they are no more exemplified than his family photos; thusly evident that his carefully prioritized values put family, the present, and the future far ahead of a reputable past with plenty of hour-long stories that only leave a small taste on the hungry tongue of curiosity.

On July 3rd, 1931, in the small country town of Corinth, Mississippi, a very particular and very reserved James Willard Brady was born, not in a hospital, but in his Mom and Dad's one room apartment which joined to their family-run gas and service station. In 1931, Corinth fulfilled all of the major stereotypes of a typical rural town: everyone seemed to know one another; many were born within the same walls that they would later live within; Main Street was composed of nothing but dirt; and, among other facets of life, people did what they could to make end's meet. With all of these "Leave it to Beaver" type qualities also came a deep, and increasingly accepted, form of racism which would remain unaccepted in the open mind and eyes of Mr. Brady throughout his life to date.

Amusingly, as Mr. Brady described his early years, Corinth was a place of old values and truly bizarre methods of entertainment. At a young age, Jim began to sell newspapers on the neighborhood street corner, and he made a profit of three cents per paper. He would occasionally meet "soldier trains" at the Corinth Train Depot which at that time, was a major railroad center. "These soldiers were always desperate for papers," Brady recalled. "I remember one specific soldier so desperate for a newspaper, he threw me a five dollar bill. Back then, five dollars was a small fortune. I threw him five to ten newspapers back, just to make sure he got one," Brady remembers, not knowing whether or not that particular soldier ended up with a newspaper. A certain, peculiar sadness seemed to overcome Brady as he told this happening. This sadness was truly intimate; the amount he cared for an unknown soldier was truly insightful.

Before having learned the true value of a dollar, James spent his first months' pay, as well as his other savings, on one of his neighbor's calves––as a pet nonetheless. By the time he recovered from his father's discipline, he had also saved up enough money to buy himself a twelve dollar, second-hand bicycle. A week later, after he then purchased a basket for the handlebars, he was able to get a paper route. His route required him to work from four o'clock to seven-thirty or so, barely making it to school each morning.

His dad was the town bailiff when he passed, but he was really an entrepreneur at heart. He owned and ran a number of small businesses and a couple of restaurants, etc., earning a modest, if any, income. Even so, he seemed to be a relatively progressive thinker. He was always trying to come up with ways to earn more money. Once, when he owned a small café, he rigged up a screen on the side of the building and charged a nickel for the silent films that he would project onto it.

James had quite a desire for law enforcement, because of his father's involvement as a constable. His father ran for sheriff almost every year James could remember. Because of Corinth's crooked political system, he was never elected. The sense of shame filled the room as James described this injustice. His dad was shot at during many of his campaigns simply because he wanted to rid Corinth of the political crookedness and the illegal gambling that was taking place.

During James's senior year in high school, he maintained contact with an FBI agent stationed in Tupelo. James's interest took him very far, as the agent from Tupelo had him set up to work for the bureau in Washington, D.C. after he graduated.

Things seemed to go down hill from there: his dad died three weeks after he graduated, which altered his decision to venture to D.C. Compounding the difficulties, his mother was in bad health, and he certainly could not leave her unattended.

After rejecting the agent's offer in D.C., James was hired at a local Machine shop, the Barry Motor Company. There he worked with hydraulic pumps, motors—just about everything that James was uninterested in at the time. He maintained his job at BMC for three years, during which he married his now long-time wife, Verna Lee.

Again the ominous clouds were moving in over Brady as BMC was shut down because of imposing unions three weeks after he had gotten married (within those weeks he had already put down payments on furniture and appliances). The plant remained closed because no one wanted anything to do with unions, which was the case for James. At this time, his mom was doing substantially better, so in order to pay off some of his down payments, James called the agent in Tupelo to inquire about his former offer. To his surprise, James was again offered to work for the F.B.I. In March of 1954, James W. Brady left Corinth with his wife Verna for D.C. and joined the Bureau.

Upon their arrival in Washington, both James and Verna were offered jobs in the main office of the Bureau. Verna began working in the card index section of the office while James headed straight to fingerprint school. There, he learned how to compare and contrast fingerprints in order to begin searching for and classifying fingerprints three months later. A few months later, he went on to teach at the very same fingerprint school.

Growing up in Corinth hampered James from ever learning how to use a typewriter which was "vital to the success of a man for the Bureau." In order to solve this problem, Mr. Brady bought himself a manual typewriter and a book from which he practiced typing every night. "I eventually got myself up to forty words per minute, which for a manual typewriter in the early 1960's," he laughed, "was something to be proud of. In approximately 1956,

Director J. Edgar Hoover, Director of the FBI, approved of filming a movie entitled *FBI Story* starring Jimmy Stewart and Vera Miles. Warner Brothers set up equipment and filmed a scene in the identification division for three days. "As far as I can recall, my friend Coleman Morton, who was later transferred to the Mobile Alabama Division, and I, were the only ones who were in the movie scene that you could recognize. And "if you blink your eyes, you missed us." We thought after three days of filming that we might have a large part in in this movie, but that was not the case. The movie was released in 1959 and had been filmed using a him this time in many other locations. We were fortunate to meet Jimmy Stewart, however we did not have opportunity to meet Ms. Miles.

After a solid stay in Washington, Jim and Verna decided they were ready to live somewhere else. Jim began inquiring about different field offices around the country, but reluctantly so as the Bureau did not take kindly to people asking to move somewhere else––Jim's subtle draw only adds to the gentility that he represented.

Jim was offered a few different jobs in the St. Louis, Indianapolis, and Memphis divisions. The former two eventually fell through (and, if his facial expressions offered any indication, he was not entirely upset), but the latter––his calling. He was offered the job at the Memphis post on a Friday at ten o'clock in the morning. In keeping with their strict stipulations, the Bureau made it clear that he had to be in his office the very next Monday at eight o'clock in the morning, sharp.

"At two minutes after ten that Friday morning, I was

out the door and on my way to rent a U-haul," Jim recalls. Jim simply threw their mattress and clothing into the back of the U-haul. Their apartment, which still included their appliances and furniture, was sold to their close friends who had been ready to buy it just in case of a situation like this one.

They arrived in Memphis on Sunday afternoon, resided in a hotel until they found an apartment later that week. Jim was immediately put on a solo night shift in which he took complaints and cases, from which he decided whether or not agents should be sent out to the scene to investigate. Jim continued to do this for another three years until he became an special investigator for the next twelve years of his life.

Jim enjoyed being an investigator and "wanted to do it for the rest of his life." He was involved with photography, fingerprinting and interviewing. The majority of his time spent as an investigator was assigned to the "Deserter Cases" and the Civil Rights Movement. These so-called "Deserter Cases" were cases in which deserters from the Millington Naval Air Station were nowhere to be found, his job was to discover their whereabouts. It became increasingly obvious that he very much enjoyed the detective aspect of his job—the smiling and laughing he enjoyed is hardly observed when talking with one about their past. He was more successful in discovering the deserters by going to their girlfriends' homes.

Investigator Jim Brady was substantially involved in the Civil Rights Movement and was assigned, among others, to the assassination of Dr. Martin Luther King, Jr. One of the first to arrive at the Lorraine Motel in downtown Memphis, James viewed the body of Dr. Martin Luther King Jr. lying on the balcony of the hotel. He then helped package James Earl Ray's rifle to be sent to Washington for fingerprinting.

A few months later, when James Meredith was the first African American to enter Ole' Mississippi University, many riots broke out. James Brady was sent to Oxford, Mississippi, for nine weeks off and on––a stretch of time he recalls as being "a war zone: the National Guard; tanks; you name it."

After his time at Oxford, Brady began driving surveillance vans for the Bureau. He entitles this portion of his life: "Where's Brady? Where's Brady?" Brady always had a suitcase packed and was always ready to leave as he was constantly asked to travel to different cities on different assignments without a moment's notice. Although this facet of an investigator's life would seem rather stressful, and indeed it was, James often enjoyed the unexpected and the unexplored.

After Jim's time spent as an investigator, he earned many letters of commendation and awards, some given by J. Edgar Hoover himself; and Jim was offered an advancement to work as an office manager. He was rather unhappy about this promotion since he had enjoyed investigating so much, but he knew he should take it because "the Bureau don't take to kindly to those who turn down promotions either." Jim disliked the notion of working under three different bosses and despised the notion of having fifty-eight employees working under him, so he decided to swim upstream and decline the advancement. Two days after James declined his promotion, an unannounced office inspection took place which resulted in a meeting between the Chief Inspector and Mr. Brady. The Chief Inspector was surprised and baffled by Brady's choice to turn down the promotion. Brady recalls the whole ordeal: "'I hear you don't want this promotion," the Chief Inspector says. "No sir, I don't", Jim says. Then, as smart as he can he says, "Then how'd you like to work as an investigator in New York City?" Jim says, "I'd like to have that office managing job if I can." "Thought so," the inspector says.

He then held this office job for fifteen years. During his tenure as head office manager, Mr. Brady proudly fabricated the "Flex-Time Program" which is still in use today. This program set up a "buddy" program so you could work flex hours together. The program basically allowed an employee to work any hours he wished as long as he worked a certain number each week. After Mr. Brady's retirement from the Bureau in 1987, he began his own work as a Private Investigator—a position he still holds today. Jim runs background checks, he still is involved in fingerprinting, and he also works on personal investigations. Jim's passion for investigation is still embedded. Currently, Mr. Brady lives a humble and happy life with his wife Verna. Mr. Brady's passions for life and for the American Dream are omnipresent even in his quiet, humble home.

What is the true measure of a man's life? Is it his education? There will always be someone with one more degree.

Is it his accomplishments in business? There will always

be someone one more rung higher on the ladder. Is it his wealth? There will always be someone richer. Perhaps really matters is this: was he a good man? Did he try every day to do the right thing? Was he a loyal, caring friend? Did he have the love of a family, and did he return that love to them in kind and more? Did he try to make the world a better place? At the end, what does a man want said about him when his family and friends step up to say their last goodbyes? That he was a smart man? That he was a rich man? That he was a powerful man? Or that he was a good man? If he is nothing else, Jim Brady is a good man.

1

Growing up in Corinth, Mississippi

At Age 14, before I was eligible to drive a truck, I was cutting wood and my dad would drive the truck to buyers who had wood burning cook stoves. After I became of age to drive, I would cut wood three days a week after school, and then deliver the wood on Saturday. This was all done after the morning paper route and school time.

One fall, I hauled cotton to the gin for two farmers who did not have time. When I was next in line, a cat jumped up on the trailer in front of me and in a flash it was sucked into the gin vacum pipe which takes the cotton bolls through a process of separating them from the cotton seeds. Needless to say, it took eight hours to repair the gin and get it in condition to running properly again.

I did not want to lose my place in line so, the only thing that I could do was sleep on my load of cotton until the gin was repaired the next morning. My parents came looking for me and brought me food. I was taught to never be idle and work hard.

I grew up in a law enforcement family and was taught honesty, fidelity, bravery, and integrity. My dad was a constable in our county. He was always considered a very honest, good person and was running for reelection at the time of his death. I would always accompany my dad to the speaking events, passing out his cards, and asking the voters for their support.

I sold newspapers on street corners as soon as I learned to make change. I saved enough money to buy a secondhand bicycle for twelve dollars, which I used on a paper route in order to make more money. I was taught to work hard and save money for basic needs such as buying my bedroom furniture and clothing..

Prior to graduation from high school, an FBI agent came to school to recruit applicants for the FBI. I wanted to go to Washington and try to qualify for a job. I filled out an application and was waiting for an answer while preparing to go to Washington. My dad passed during this time and my mother had health issues. Since I was an only child., I had to call the agent and explain I could not go to Washington. He advised that if things got better for us, to call him. He would see what he could do to reinstate the application.

In the meantime, I obtained a job at Berry Motor Company in Corinth, Mississippi, learning to make hydraulic motors and lifts. I thought it would be a stable job, and Verna Lee Cartwright,my girl friend of approximately two years,and I would get married. We planned to remodel our house into a duplex, my mother on one side and Verna and I on the other.

We did marry on November 12, 1953. Two weeks before Christmas, Mr. Berry, who owned the machine shop, closed the plant. He informed me, confidentially, that if the workers continued to try to form a union for his plant he would never open the plant again.

Verna Lee and I had finished remodeling the home and bought new furniture. We were planning to be in Corinth the rest of our life. Jobs in Corinth were very scarce, and since my mother's health had improved, and the holidays were over, we agreed we would have to relocate to get a job.

I called the FBI agent from Tupelo, Mississippi and talked to him about resubmitting the application for the FBI, since it had been three years since I originally applied. He told me to meet him at the police department in Corinth on Sunday afternoon at three in the afternoon. Verna Lee went with me. During the interview, he questioned us about what she was going to do when we got to Washington. I informed him that we both would have to work to pay bills that had accumulated since our marriage. He asked if we just wanted a job, or did we want a career? I informed him that I wanted a career, and I did not like the idea of moving from job to job. He stated, "Then why don't I send an application for Verna Lee as well."

He did send the applications. Approximately six weeks later an appointment letter came for both of us to report to Washington DC on March 29, 1954. I had applied for a position in finger prints which required extensive classroom work before actually searching for subjects, identifying or comparing prints. Verna was assigned to the correspondence unit of the Identification Division of the FBI.

Jim - Age 8

2

Falling in Love with Verna

Before the beginning of my senior year of school, a family moved to Corinth from Walnut, Mississippi, and moved to within five houses from my family's house. I noticed the new girl many times in passing and while going to school and finally got the opportunity to ask her if she would like a ride, since I was driving because my dad wanted me to leave school early to help him work. Her name was Verna Lee Cartwright, and we had not spoken to each other before. It looked like it was starting to rain, and I thought since most everyone in school knew me, it would be a nice thing to do to ask her to ride.

However, in a sarcastic way, she said, "No, thank you. I'll walk."

Her attitude startled me, and I replied, "Oh, that's all right. I thought if you wanted to ride, you could get a stick horse," and I drove away.

In a few weeks, we met again through mutual friends, and we started dating, which lasted through her senior year, at which time she went to Memphis, Tennessee, to the Baptisl Hospital School of Nursing. She decided it was best for us to break up, since we were never able to see each other because of our schedules.

We were apart for more than two years. After she finished school, she came back to Corinth and we got back to dating. We got married on November 12, 1953.

Since my dad had passed away only three weeks after I graduated and it looked as though I needed to care for my mother, I renovated my house into a duplex so that Mother would have her privacy, and we would have ours. Verna and I bought new furniture. including a bedroom suite, a living room sofa and tables, an electric stove, a refrigerator, and other items necessary for the house.

3

Headed for FBI School in Washington DC

Over the three year period, my mother's health improved and I called the agent in Tupelo, Mississippi, who discussed the possibility of reinstating the application. The agent instructed me to meet him at the Corinth Police Dept on Sunday afternoon.

I informed him that Verna would have to work and she would start applying. He stated that he would send applications for both of us. We were both accepted to work with the FBI and instructed to report March 27, 1954.

I was assigned to Ident Division Fingerprrint school, learning to classify, and identify fingerprints. As time passed I learned to take prints from individuals, both live and deceased. Next, I learned to photograph fingerprints at a crime scene and also lift the prints from objects.

Verna was assigned to the correspondence and index sections. She would answer inquiries from other agencies as well as record their communications.

Since we had no children, during the time she was employed at the defense department we adopted a wonderful son, He was very intelligent and always trained himself to being a doctor. While attending Rhodes College in Memphis, he approached me one day and stated that he would like to talk. He said that he hoped that I would not be discouraged with him, but he had changed his mind about being a doctor. I was afraid that he was going to tell me that he wanted to be a truck driver or something. I asked him what he wanted to do—*and he said that he wanted to be a dentist*! With great relief, I told him to go after it and work hard, which he did for thirty years. Nineteen months after adopting Stan, our second son,Steve, was born. He and Stan were always very close as brothers. We had friends who had a son, Keith Haney, about four years older than Stan All the young men were very much interested in law enforcement. One day I took the boys to the FBI Office for a tour. From that time forward, the boys were pro law enforcement.

Keith continued his path to law enforcement and retired from the Metro PD as a Lieutenant and opened his private investigative agency and employs over twelve people. Steve is currently a Sargent with the warrant division, and has eight employees. Steve is now eligible to retire.!

FBI Academy

4

Assignments – Memphis FBI office

Assignment – Memphis, Tennessee
1960–1980
FBI Bureau

In 1957, I was a fingerprint instructor with eight students in the fingerprint section. There were 20 million fingerprint cards on file and an average of 3,300 wanted subjects identified. Included in the criminal database were fingerprints from 73,000 suspected terrorists processed by the US or International law enforcement agencies who work with us. The first use of computers to search fingerprints files took place in October 1980. Prior to this, they were identified b By using a special magnifying glass and using our natural eyes to identify the fingerprints by the ridges which is in each persons hands and toes of the feet which are different in every person.

One Friday, I was notified of my transfer and was ordered to be in Memphis at 8 am on the following Monday, and then promoted to the security patrol on night shift. At the Memphis Division, I was assigned to the Chief Clerk's office for a few weeks while I learned the operation of a field office. The desk and chairs were very old and made of wood. The Bureau cars were black four door sedans with black wall tires which made the cars stand out as law enforcement vehicles. All cars did not have AM radios, no air, no power steering or brakes. It was mandatory that the personnel out of the office contact the office every hour, therefore, necessary to have two-way radios in the Bureau cars. However, all cars did not have them so it was necessary to stop and insert a dime in a pay phone or borrow the phone from some service station or business. After training and working the night shifts alone for approximately three years, I started getting cases assigned to me and I was promoted to special investigator. I was instructed that if I was alerted by radio of a bank robbery, I should drop everything and travel to the scene.

This was the most interesting and satisfying job because I only had to report to the *Special Agent in Charge*, although the cases and assignments were received from other agents and supervisors. I was assigned to all deserter cases including the Millington Naval Air Station. The most cases I was assigned was 62 in one month count. I performed these duties under the direction of many SAC and supervisors and received many letters of commendation and incentive awards.

In 1972, I was appointed office manager. One accomplishment, which the Bureau is still enforcing to date, was the Flex Time System. This allows employees to adjust their work hours with a buddy system in order to have coverage in all necessary jobs 24 hours per day. If an employee needed to come in late because of a doctor or dentist appointment, his buddy could cover for him and he could work late to make it up, thus saving sick leave or annual leave. The Bureau approved this system in the late 1970s.

The Memphis Division investigated it's most famous case, the assassination of Dr. Martin Luther King, Junior. In April 1968, Dr. King had stopped in Memphis to support a sanitary worker strike for improved treatment. While standing on the balcony of the Loraine Motel, King was shot by James Earl Ray a known racist with a lengthy criminal record. Memphis agents responded immediately, tracking down clues that pinpointed Ray as the culprit. Agents determined that Ray, using an alias had purchased a rifle and rented a hotel room near the crime scene. Agents also found his fingerprints on a rifle. With the assistance of Scotland Yard, the FBI tracked down Ray in London two months later. He initially confessed to the assassination, possibly to avoid the death penalty, then recanted and claimed he was set up by a mysterious individual. The Department of Justice reviewed this conspiracy theory but found no evidence of others being involved.

Located in another chapter of this book is a complete story of James Meredith being led by the chief of the civil rights division and the director of the United States Marshals into Ole Miss University to register as a student. This turned into a tremendous battle where two people were killed and over 40 were wounded. This event occurred in September 1963.

In the 1970s, Memphis also worked a case that would

be significant to 14 innovations invoice identification and corroborations and the first use of these techniques in federal court. The investigation centered on professional bank extortionist who had extorted over $500,000 in 20 schemes across the nation. Their luck ran out in Memphis in 1976, when they threatened to bring harm to the bankers family and bomb his bank. Quick-acting agents collect the pair retrieving $100,000 payoff from the banker. Voice identifications nail of the extortionist by identifying them as a source of the threats. FBI headquarters noted that the techniques Memphis applied would promptly solve 30 similar pending cases and countless more in the future.

The Memphis Division handled other financial industry related crimes as well. The City of Memphis was world's third-largest municipal bond center, so the office remained busy chasing check kiters and other white-collar criminals. In one late 1970s investigation, agents uncovered evidence that LOC industries was running a multi-million dollar scheme to fraudulently sell more than 1000 distributorships and bilk victims (mainly small businesses) out of $50,000 to $70,000 per day.

Bank robberies were also a serious concern for the division at this time. During the mid-1970s, the Dawson gang pulled 30 heist across the southeastern United States, each robbery yielding between 50 and $100,000. The gang wore ski mask and jumpsuits, carried semi automatic rifles, bushmaster pistols, and assaulted bank employees as they committed their robberies. FBI Memphis and other southeastern offices spent many hours trying to catch the gang they finally did following the robbery of the McEwing bank in Memphis. Although the gang got away with more than $59,000, law enforcement was close on their tail following the robbery. The criminals hid in nearby woods, but local authorities and Memphis agents brought in tracking dogs and quickly pinpointed their location. A gunfight ensued, but the firepower of the agents and police forced the gang to surrender.

Another significant area of crime for Memphis Division was public corruption. In the late 1970's the office began receiving calls from state and local government officials about corruption issues. These tips led to several of Memphis area Sheriff's and Deputies being convicted of taking payoffs for not forcing state and local liquor laws. In another investigation code-name SHELBCO (short for Shelby County case), county and city employees were convicted for giving public works construction and paving contracts to select contractors in exchange for payoffs and Christmas gifts.

In the coming decade, the number of corruption cases grew more widespread and began to reach higher levels of government, even touching Tennessee Gov. Leonard Ray Blanton and members of his administration. In 1980, Blanton and two of his cronies were indicted for their roles in a scheme to provide liquor license to those who agreed to pay a portion of their profits for the license. Another serious investigation involving Blanton and his cronies was TENNPAR (Short for Tennessee pardon), which investigated the large-scale illegal release of serious offenders from the state penitentiary by the state parole board in exchange for bribes Blanton was convicted and sentenced to prison. Details of this investigation may be found in the book "FBI code-name 10 par," by Hank Hillin, who led the investigation and wrote the book.

During the 1980s, Memphis ran operation Rocky top with the Tennessee Bureau of investigation and the IRS. This joint effort found the illegalities and bribery among charity bingo operators, lobbyist, regulators, and state legislators. By the end of the operation, more than 50 individuals including state legislators were convicted. FBI Memphis also handling other types of investigation. In one operation, agents discovered that the national coal exchange was operating nationwide organized boiler rooms selling coal contracts without the raw supplies to back them up. Hundreds of investors committed millions of dollars to phantom commodities. Following division's investigation, dozens of subjects plead guilty, and local fines reached $150,000. The IRS and the US attorney's office estimated that the case save the government $5 million in lost revenue from an illegal tax shelter and $25 million in potential economic losses. Intelligence developed during the investigation resulted in numerous other investigations.

In one mid-1980s case worked with Memphis Police Department, the Division investigated two partners who operated a fictitious chop shop targeting commercialized auto stripping. Investigators uncovered 21 chop shops in Tennessee and Arkansas and arrested 146 individuals, 120 of whom were convicted. The case also led to the recovery of 265 vehicles valued at $3.6 million, stolen parts were worth more than $100,000, 1300 pounds of stolen dynamite, 166 pounds of marijuana, automatics and other weapons.

FBI Criminal History
Memphis Tennessee

In the late 1960s, the division worked a number of cases involving cotton for production, a vital industry in the Memphis area. Since cotton's quality and value deteriorated over time, the grading of cotton stock was crucial, and fraudulently graded cotton could cost the federal government up to $15 per bail. In 1967, the Memphis division learned that a cotton company purchase sure was paying bribes so that 14,000 bales would be improperly downgraded. Agents conducted exhaustive interviews and physical surveillance, leading to the arrest of a dozen US Department of agriculture employees and cotton buyers on bribery and fraud charges. The divisions thorough investigation saved the US government $200,000 and heightened awareness of need for stringent monitoring of potential fraud.

The next year, the Memphis Division investigated it's most famous case, the assassination of Dr. Martin Luther King, Junior. In April 1968, Dr. King had stopped in Memphis to support a sanitary worker strike for improved treatment. While standing on the balcony of the Lorraine motel, King was shot by James Earl Ray a known racist with a lengthy criminal record. Memphis agents responded immediately, tracking down clues that pinpointed Ray as the culprit. Agents determined that Ray, using an alias had purchased a rifle and rented a hotel room near the crime scene. Agents also found his fingerprints on a rifle. With the assistance of Scotland Yard, the FBI tracked down Ray in London two months later. He initially confessed to the assassination, possibly to avoid the death penalty, then recanted and claimed he was set up by a mysterious individual. The Department of Justice reviewed this conspiracy theory but found no evidence of others being involved.

Located in another chapter of this book is a complete story of James Meredith being led by the chief of the civil rights division and the director of the United States Marshals into Ole Miss University to register as a student. This turned into a tremendous battle where two people were killed and over 40 were wounded. This event occurred in September 1963.

In the 1970s, Memphis also work a case that would be significant 14 innovations invoice identification and corroboration and the first use of these techniques in federal court. The investigation centered on professional bank extortionist who had extorted over $500,000 in 20 schemes across the nation. Their luck ran out in Memphis in 1976, when they threatened to bring harm to the bankers family and bomb his bank. Quick-acting agents collect the pair retrieving $100,000 payoff from the banker. Voice identifications nail of the extortionist by identifying them as a source of the threats. FBI headquarters noted that the techniques Memphis applied would promptly solve 30 similar pending cases and countless more in the future.

The Memphis Division handled other financial industry related crimes as well. The City of Memphis was world's third-largest municipal bond center, so the office remained busy chasing check hiders and other white-collar criminals in one late 1970s investigation, agents uncovered evidence that LOC industries was running a multimillion dollar scheme to fraudulently sell more than 1000 distributorships and bilk victims (mainly small businesses) out of $50,000 to $70,000 per day.

Bank robberies were also a serious concern for the division at this time. During the mid-1970s, the Dawson gang pulled a 30 highest across the southeastern United States, each robbery yielding between 50 and $100,000. The gang wore ski mask and jumpsuits, carried semi automatic rifles, bushmaster pistols, and assaulted bank employees as they committed their robberies. FBI Memphis and other southeastern offices spent many hours trying to catch the gang they finally did following the robbery of the McEwing bank in Memphis. Although the gang got away with more than $59,000, law enforcement was close on their tail following the robbery. The criminals hid in nearby woods, but local authorities and Memphis agents brought in tracking dogs and quickly pinpoint their location. A gunfight ensued, but the firepower of the agents and police forced the gang to surrender.

Another significant area of crime for Memphis Division was public corruption. In the late 1970's the office began receiving a number of calls from state and local government officials about corruption issues. These tips led to a number of Memphis area Sheriff's and Deputies being convicted of taking payoffs for not forcing state and local liquor laws. In another investigation codename SHELBCO (short for Shelby County case), county and city employees were convicted for giving public works construction and paving contracts to select contractors in exchange for payoffs and Christmas gifts.

In the coming the decade, the number of corruption cases grew more widespread and began to reach higher levels of government, even touching Tennessee Gov. Leonard Ray Blanton and members of his administration. In 1980, Blanton and two of his age were indicted for their roles in a scheme to provide liquor license to those who agreed to pay a portion of their profits for the license. Another serious investigation involving Blanton and his cronies was TENNPAR (Short for Tennessee pardon), which investigated the large-scale illegal release of serious offenders from the state penitentiary by the state parole board in exchange for bribes Blanton was convicted and sentenced to prison. Details of this investigation may be found in the book "FBI codename 10 par," by Hank Hillin, who led the investigation and wrote the book.

During the 1980s, Memphis ran operation Rocky top with the Tennessee Bureau of investigation and the IRS. This joint effort found the illegalities and bribery among charity bingo operators, lobbyist, regulators, and state legislators. By the end of the operation, more than 50 individuals including state legislators were convicted. FBI Memphis also handling other types of investigation. In one operation, agents discovered that the national coal exchange was operating nationwide organized boiler rooms selling coal contracts without the raw supplies to back them up. Hundreds of investors committed millions of dollars to phantom commodities. Following division's investigation, dozens of subjects pled guilty, and local fines reached $150,000. The IRS and the US attorney's office estimated that the case save the government $5 million in lost revenue from a illegal tax shelter and $25 million in potential economic losses. Intelligence developed during the investigation resulted in numerous other investigations.

One of the best Judges, in my opinion, was on the bench one day when we had charged this old man, in his late seventies, with 4 counts of interstate transportation of stolen motor vehicles and he was next on the docket. The judge looked over his small glasses at the man and stated "I am so tired seeing you in my court for car thefts, I am giving you twenty years". The old man said, "oh, judge, You can't do that, I may not live that long." Judge replied, "Well, you just do the best that you can."

5

FBI Director J. Edgar Hoover gets involved

In 1956, the FBI Director, J. Edgar Hoover, gave approval for Warner Brothers to film "The FBI Story" starring Jimmy Stewart and Vera Miles. Warner Brothers set up equipment and filmed a scene in the Identification Division, in Washington for three days and as far as I can recall, my friend Coleman Morton and I were the only ones identifiable in the movie after it's release in 1959. We thought after three days of filming that we might have a large part in the movie, however, when the movie was released, if you blinked your eyes you would have missed us. The movie had been shot in several locations and other divisions as well. We were fortunate to meet Jimmy Stewart, however, we didn't have the opportunity to meet Vera Miles.

Director

6

Russians are here

Back in the late 50's, the Bureau had no cell phones and the rule was that the office would be covered 24 hours per day and never left unattended. One night when I was on duty alone, I received a call from the agents in Nashville who were trailing Russians coming from Oak Ridge, Tennessee, the site of a major nuclear weaons facility The Bureau rule was that any foreign officials would be trailed to determine their contacts and purpose of visiting. The agents stated that they were traveling through Nashville and would recontact me when they reached Jackson, Tennessee. At the time of arriving in Jackson, they passed through and were headed to Memphis, Tennessee.

I immediately called SAC and woke him up at approximately 1:30 am, advising him of the situation and to get instructions as to who he would like to take over the surveillance as the Russians entered the Memphis area. As I was describing the situation to him, he started to snore. I was talking as loud as I could to wake him up, however, I heard the phone hit the floor.

I was now in a situation that I did not want to be in,

but knew that I could not leave the office nor was there any way that I knew to possibly wake him up. I decided to go ahead and call the security agents and wake them up and advise them that the SAC wanted the situation covered immediately and for them to meet the Nashville agents at a given point and take over the surveillance. Needless to say they were not too happy about having to get up and go out to work at two or 3 o'clock in the morning.

The next morning at approximately 9:00 am, while I was sleeping, I received a phone call from the SAC asking if I had called him the night before. I advised him of the situation and who I had assigned the surveillance to. He stated, "Oh, I knew you would handle it." I asked him to be sure that the Agents did not find out that he did not give the order for them to handle the surveillance because they would be very unhappy to know that I made that decision without the SAC's approval. He stated "No Problem".

7

Robert Kennedy wants me fired

In the early 1960s during the Civil Rights era, the Memphis Division of the FBI was periodically assigned to work with John Doar, the Assistant Attorney General of the Civil Rights Division of the Department of Justice in Mississippi photographing election law records.

This was a time before the Jackson Mississippi Division of the FBI was opened and the New Orleans FBI office covered the southern part of Mississippi, and Memphis covered the northern part of Mississippi. After working with Mr. Doar on several different occasions, he would request me to meet him in Mississippi to assist him.

He requested me to meet him in Greenwood, Mississippi and one night around midnight he knocked on my motel door and was very excited. I ask what the trouble was and he verified that he had heard of a planned march on the main street with a group of Blacks going east and the Ku Klux Klan going west at noon the next day. He stated that this March has to be stopped, or we will have the biggest war of the South here. He instructed me that he wanted me to immediately advise the sheriff to stop the march. I advised Mr. Doar that I would locate the sheriff and tell him that Mr. Doar had heard of a planned march for noon the next day, however, I was not going to tell the sheriff that he had to stop the march, because the FBI had no authority to tell the sheriff how to run his county unless there was a federal violation, which there was not.

Mr. Doar became very upset and advised me that I was there to assist him and if I did not follow orders that he would have my job tomorrow morning. I told him that I was very sorry that he saw it that way, but I was not going to tell the sheriff to stop the march. At that point Mr. Doar left my room. I did tell the sheriff about Mr. Doar's rumors of the march, however I did not mention Mr. Doar's instructions to me.

When I returned to the motel, I thought I should advise the SAC in Memphis of Mr. Doar's intention of calling the Atty. Gen. Robert Kennedy and requesting that I be fired. I awoke the SAC in Memphis, Tennessee and informed him of the situation. He said, "you don't really think he will do that do you"? I said, "if I was a betting man, I would bet everything I have that he would because I was with him all day every day and he calls Bobby Kennedy three or four times a day and they are very, very close."

The SAC instructed that I stay in my room until he called me the next morning after he called our director Mr. J. Edgar Hoover. At approximately 7:30 AM central time the SAC called me and stated that I was right. Mr. Doar had called Bobby Kennedy and recommended that I be fired because of insubordination. I stated, "well I guess you want me to bring the car and equipment back to Memphis."

The SAC stated, "don't you want to know what Mr. Hoover said?", I said, " I sure would like to know." He said, "Mr. Hoover told Bobby Kennedy to run the Attorney General office and he would run the FBI. However, he did tell me to get you out of Mississippi without Doar."

I told him that order was like getting a raise to get away from Mr. Doar and out of Mississippi at that time. I asked him if he wanted me to tell Mr. Doar that I was leaving to which he answered "I don't care what you tell him." I left and did not say anything to Mr. Doar. I never saw Mr. Doar again.

8

The VP Banker Who embezzled

One afternoon at approximately 1:00 pm, an alert was received regarding a bank robbery on Highway 61 in Memphis, Tennessee. I immediately realized that I was the first of the Bureau to arrive at the bank. The Bank guard was standing at the back entrance allowing no one to leave until they were interviewed. Upon the arrival at the bank, the FBI bank robbery coordinator was attempting to start an interview with the bank manager in a private room.

As other Agents arrived and began interviewing the tellers and customers, determined that no one knew anything about the bank being robbed, In the 1960's, when law enforcement agencies could get information from credit bureaus, I called the Credit Bureau regarding the manager of the bank. From the record of the manager, he owed more money each month and the total amounted to more than he could ever hope to pay.

I knocked on the door where the F.B.I. coordinator was interviewing the bank manager and motioned for the coordinator to come out. I informed him of my findings and told him that he had the subject. He instructed for us to finish as if nothing found and meet back at the office at 4 pm.

As this case unfolded, it was determined that the bank manager was going to have an audit the next day and he realized that he could not replace the $40,000.00 which he had embezzled over a period of time. The Federal Judge back in those days who gave him a 20 year sentence.

The bank manager also had a wife and three children, in addition to a girlfriend who he could not afford.

Upon further investigation, the girl friend was located in Millington, Tn., also working in a bank. When asked about the character of the subject, she admitted that they were dating and that he was getting a divorce from his wife and he was going to marry her. She stated that he was a good Christian gentleman and well liked at the banks.

When asked if she ever spent the night with him in a motel, she became very upset and replying that she was not that type girl and didn't appreciate the incinuation that she would do it.

I ask her who she thought the girl was with him on a certain date in the Holiday Inn on Hwy 61. She began crying and begging us not to tell her parents. I told her that we definitely would not tell her parents however, they would hear it in the court room.

9

A Killer - "you have tricked me"

In 1962, the FBI office in Memphis opened a case charging a subject with unlawful flight to avoid prosecution for murder. The case originated in South Carolina and the subject was believed to be in the Memphis area. Between South Carolina and Memphis, he had killed and buried 6 or 7 bodies. However, the original charge of murder was placed in Columbia, South Carolina. Most of the bodies were young children.. After extensive investigation by the Memphis office and West Memphis Resident Agency Office, a subject was located. He was brought in to the Memphis Division Agency Office for questioning several times, however the US attorney advised that we did not have enough evidence to make the charge stick. The first time that he was in the office. The case agent ask me to photograph and fingerprint him for elimination purposes. We talked as I fingerprinted him and gave me his phone number so that I might call him in case I have a question about someone in South Carolina. I told him that we really appreciated his cooperation, in trying to gain his confidence. He and I communicated several times when

I could obtain a few new photos of criminals and other individuals to see if he could identify. He informed me that he was teaching piano lessons to children in West Memphis, Arkansas, and he would be available any day after students were dismissed.

The US Attorney gave the order we had enough evidence to make the murder charge and we should pick him up and proceed to extradite him back to Columbia, South Carolina. The SAC immediately called a conference and started laying out plans for the apprehension of the subject after he dismissed his class of students at 4 pm. After all the assignments had been made by the SAC, I asked if I might ask him just one thing.

"With your permission, I will call the subject and ask him to come to the office and no one will have to leave the office in Little Rock or have to do anything except the West Memphis agent". The SAC stated that he might get suspicious and leave and he did not think that was a good idea. Another agent told SAC that if anyone could do it, Brady could. The majority thought it would work and convinced the SAC. I called the subject and asked him if he could come to the office because I have some new photos for him to observe. He agreed and at 5:15 pm, he appeared and I had a 5 x 7 picture of the subject on the last page. When he turned to that page, he yelled "that's me!!!" I said that's right and it is all over. He said "You have tricked me". I immediately left the room while his rights were being read and other processing.

This was a very satisfying achievement to be involved with and one of my greatest accomplishments.

DOESN'T PAY TO GET UP SOME DAYS

One Friday afternoon in one of the northern divisions of Nebraska, a couple of agents had big plans for a family party and cookout that night. It was in the middle of the afternoon and they had just finished an interview and were saying that they sure hoped that no bank robbery would occur and ruin their plans for the night.

The agents were out in the country on the main highway when an announcement of bank robbery came over the radio about 3 p.m.

The agents decided that they would patrol the highway in case a lead came that way. They noticed a trail at the end of a corn row that led to a large wooded area and they decided to pull into the wooded area and wait for other broadcast. As they pulled in to the area and cut the engine off, the back door of the Bureau car opened and an individual jumped in the back seat with the bank money in a bag. The agents looked at each other and at the bank robber and stated "it doesn't pay to get up somedays".

The bank robber had arrived at the location on a motorcycle and now they had to wait for the pickup car to come to pick up the robber with the money. When the pickup car did arrive, it was the same type and color car as the Bureau car.

The agents then had to arrest the pickup driver as well as the individual with the money and as it turned out these two agents were the only ones that had to work late because of the bank robbery.

k4634183 www.fotosearch.com

10

Wil James Meredith go college

In September 1963, at Ole Miss University in Oxford, MS, the United States Marshalls, led by Director James McShane and Department of Justice Civil Rights Leader, John Doar, were preparing to escort Meredith into the school for registration on the following Monday morning. Meredith had previously been denied registration.

The Memphis Division of the FBI covered the northern part of Mississippi and New Orleans covered the southern part prior to opening the Jackson, MS office of the FBI. The Bureau had previously set up a temporary office in the Namath Motel on Highway 6 going into Oxford near the University. A straight line telephone into the Memphis Office had been installed and was attended around the clock at both locations.

Agents were being dispatched from all near by offices including Nashville and the SAC ordered me to pick up SA'S Hank Hillin and Billy Sheets at the Memphis Airport and drive them to Oxford.

As we arrived, I heard gun shots nearby and it became more intensified by the minute, There were News Media and Television Equipment in front of the Lyceum Building. One Marshall's car and a WMPS News Truck were over turned and burned.

Many reports from people listening to radios in Memphis and other locations state they could hear gun fire on the radio.

Governor Ross Barnett had sent the Mississippi National Guard and Highway Patrol to the site to prevent violence and also to prevent Meredith from entering the University. Governor Barnett also sent Lt. Governor Paul Johnson to lead the states operation. As the evening grew near, the crowd became more rowdy and also grew in numbers.

McShane ordered the Marshals to fire Tear Gas which started people firing all types of guns and ammunition. The firing continued all night, two people were killed and over forty US Marshals were wounded.

The following morning McShane, Doar and Meredith arrived at the building to register Meredith and were met by Lt. Gov. Johnson, the Highway Patrol and some National Guardsmen, They were refused admittance.

Back in Jackson, the Governor was on the phone with President Kennedy about the situation. Some results of the conversation were President Kennedy ordered 36,000 National Guardsmen to Oxford immediately.

Meredith was admitted to the University with the aid of the National Guard and John Doar.

On the following day after that Sunday night when two people were killed and over 40 were wounded, all of the guns which were confiscated by the FBI and Marshals were loaded into two cars. I drove one carrying 156 guns and the other number unknown.

The guns were prepared in Memphis for shipping to the FBI lab for examination and comparison to the bullets which killed the two people on the Ole Miss campus.

I never learned the result of the tests.

After a lapse of nine or ten weeks, I was reporting to work in the Memphis Office and SAC dessly summoned me to his office. He handed me a teletype to read which instructed the SAC to send someone to the Howard Johnson Motel to pick up the director of the marshals, James McShane, who was using the name of James Martin and escort him to the federal building in Oxford, MS. I inquired why the FBI was escorting McShane when he had agents located in the same building with the FBI. SAC stated that he did not know, however this was the orders from FBI headquarters and you handle it.

I thought that I would have Mr. McShane talking and find out why the FBI was escorting him instead of his marshals. However, everytime I would mention something which would lead into a conversation about Oxford on our trip, Mr. McShane would change the subject. As we arrived in front of the Federal Building, which was also the Post Office, there were numerous news and television media in front. Mr. McShane asked if I knew how to get to the back door of the building.

As we arrived and before the car completely stopped, Mr. McShane got out of the car and ran into the back door of the bldg.. We were the only people in site in the corridor until Sheriff Ford of Oxford came walking toward us in the long corridor.

I spoke to the Sheriff because I knew him personally and he also spoke and looked at McShane and said "Mr. McShane", which he answered, "Yes," I am Sheriff Ford and as he handed him a warrant, he told him that he was under arrest.

I informed the Sheriff that I brought him in and asked if I was also under arrest. He ssaid "No," but I needed to come into the room for preliminary procedures to begin. As we entered the room, there was state attorneys, Lt Governor Johnson, U.S. Dept of Justice Attorneys. Chief of Civil Rights, John Doar and others.

I asked the Sheriff if I could make a phone call which after about 20 minutes he took me to a private room where I called the office at the motel and informed Agent Sheets, he held me on the phone while he rang Memphis on the Hot Line.

When he contacted the ASAC (Halter), he instructed Sheets to "Send two agents over there and get Brady out of there and have him call me".

After the ASAC called the Bureau Headquarters and conferred about why the FBI was involved with this operation on this date, it was determined that since there was a warrant for the arrest of director McShane if he ever entered the State of Mississippi, they did not want him to be identified until he had officially arrived and in the State's custody.

(I was later informed that they were also afraid of an assassination attempt.)

Rioting during Civil Rights era

11

Who Stole the $50000 1940 LaSalle

In mid summer of 1965, two of my close friends owned a service station and repair shop in Memphis, Tennessee. One of the men had purchased a 1940 LaSalle and restored it to appear showroom new. The car was valued at over $50,000.

The owner was preparing to close the station one night to go home in this vehicle, he thought he saw a movement in the station and backed up leaving the key in and the motor running. He stepped inside the building, not out of sight of the car, and as he turned to returned to the car, he saw it drive out of the driveway and toward the Expressway. He immediately called me at home. I told him to call the Highway Patrol and Police Department immediately and I would be on the way to his house. I asked him to get a photograph of the car, take it to the auto traders magazine which would come out in a couple of days and get them to put the picture with a note that there would be a reward for information that would lead to the recovery of the car on the front cover of the magazine.

Then I called the supervisor of the interstate

transportation of stolen motor vehicles and asked him if we could open a case on this stolen car. He advised that we could not open the case until we had evidence that the car had crossed the state line.

As time continued to pass and it appeared no one with the Police or Highway Patrol had received any information regarding the vehicle, the hope of recovery was diminishing.

It was approximately two weeks before Christmas of the same year our friends' daughter called me, very excited, and said that she had just received a phone call asking to speak to her dad. Her parents at that time were visiting friends approximately 15 miles from home. She stated that the caller stated that he would call back in one hour and advise them where the car was located. I told her that she needed to call her parents immediately and to tell them also that I was on the way to their home.

When the call came through, I asked my friend to answer the call and I would listen; and for him to try not to upset the caller. The caller instructed for him to listen because he was only going to repeat it one time. He stated that the 1940 LaSalle which was stolen from his service station was now parked at the New Orleans airport in New Orleans, Louisiana under a green canopy. At this point the caller hung up.

I immediately called the Memphis FBI office and ask them to open a new case on this stolen vehicle. Then I called the New Orleans FBI office, giving them the Memphis case number and asked them to check the New Orleans airport with the New Orleans Police and see if they could locate the 1940 LaSalle under a green canopy. In approximately three hours, the New Orleans office contacted the Memphis office and advised the 1940 LaSalle had been located and was parked near a fence at the New Orleans airport with a green tarp over it. It appeared to be in good shape and not wrecked. At that point the owner called the Memphis airport and made arrangements to fly to New Orleans to retrieve his car. After examining the car the owner could only find one scratch where someone had tried to raise the hood of the engine.

He drove the car from New Orleans to Memphis and stated that it was in perfect shape. My friend was a very, very, happy man and his family had a very Merry Christmas.

12

Church Bombings in the South

In a small Mississippi town, on Sunday night1968, while a black church service was in process; the building did not have air conditioning nor did it have screens over the windows.

An object came through the open window which was shaped like a Coca-Cola can and had a homemade lever from the top down the side similar to a hand grenade. The object rolled from the window area to the front of the pulpit.

There was an elderly lady always sitting on the front row in front of the pulpit. The little lady hobbled up and picked it up and threw it back out the window.

The FBI office was notified of the incident the next morning. An older agent and I were assigned to go to the town and do some interviews to see what facts we could find regarding the attempt, apparently, to do damage to this church.

After several interviews with different people near the church, it was determined that one individual living a few doors behind the church, did, in fact pick the object up and was believed to have taken it home with him. He was very cooperative and stated that he did bring the object home and has it sitting on his mantle in his home. He got the object and brought it outside for us to observe. Upon looking at this can closely, we determined that the pin holding the handle was halfway out and we could not tell if this was a real explosive or a dummy.

The senior agent had to make a decision of what to do with the object, so he suggested that I take it to Millington Naval Air Station and let the crew test to see if it was a real bomb or dummy.

I thanked him very much for pulling rank on me and I would do the best I could to see him back at the office. He had to stay and do more interviews and I understood.

I stopped at Walmart and bought some cushions and straps to secure this object in case I had a wreck or that the pin would come out on the way to Millington.

I met with the security officer in charge at Millington and he assigned a couple of servicemen to take the object to a secure vat to determine if it was live or not.

We were standing outside the building when we heard a loud explosion. The officer looked at me and said, "I am glad that you did not have a wreck".

13

Crooks fraudulently graded cotton

In the late 1960s, the division worked a number of cases involving cotton for production, a vital industry in the Memphis area. Since cotton's quality and value deteriorated over time, the grading of cotton stock was crucial, and fraudulently graded cotton could cost the federal government $15 per bale. In 1967, the Memphis Division learned that a cotton company purchase sure was paying bribes so that 14,000 bales would be improperly downgraded. Agents conducted exhaustive interviews and physical surveillance, leading to the arrest of a dozen US Department of Agriculture employees and cotton buyers on bribery and fraud charges. The divisions thorough investigation saved the United States government $200,000 and heightened awareness of need for stringent monitoring of potential fraud.

14

The FBI staff visits the Grand Ole Opry

Interesting
Bureau Facts

During the year 1969 SA Hank Hillin and and Jim Brady discussed getting a group together for a weekend in Nashville, Tennessee., and after having a banquet, going to the grand Ole Opry. After advising everyone in the Memphis division., approximately 56 employees and family members decided to attend.

It was a very enjoyable weekend and many others who did not attend asked us to do it again and they would like to attend.

SA Hillin stated that he could not assist in planning another event due to the time required in planning.

In a conversation with director of the FBI, Clarence Kelly, I mentioned to him that with his permission to use Bureau communications and duplicating equipment, I would continue this event and call it "FBI family weekend in Nashville", pointing out that since employees were transferred often and lose contact with many friends who they had worked with in years past, this would be a way to maintain contact with friends in the Bureau and making new friends in the Bureau.

He was very interested and said that he and his wife would attend. Approximately one week prior to the event he call me in Memphis stating that he would not be able to attend however, Mr. Lee Colwell, the Executive Assistant Director, and his wife would be attending the event.

Mr. Colwell and his wife did attend and were very impressed with the banquet and also the backstage tour of the grand old Opry as well as all functions planned for the weekend.

I received letters from both Mr. Kelly and Mr. Colwell, commending me for organizing this event and having different Opry artist attend and perform for the group.

This event continued for 15 years and until Brady retired in December 1986. We averaged approximately 200 in attendance and the most was 426.

Following are various photos of Bureau personnel attending a banquet and then the Opry and some photos of Bureau employees backstage with Opry artist.

The FBI Academy

FBI - Staff visits and employees visit Grand Ole Opry

Verna and Agent Barter & wife with other visiting
Earnest Tubb back
_____ Opry

15

Lasting memories

I became 32° Mason of the Memphis Lodge and have attended the grand Lodge for many years. I was very fortunate in having a part in the induction of Little Jimmy Dickens of the Grand Ole Opry into the Tennessee Masonic Lodge.

In the mid seventies, there was a concert with the Statler Brothers and Barbara Mandrell Booked for the Memphis Coliseum.

The personnel in the security office of the coliseum were always very nice to allow me backstage at the Coliseum and I would always stand out of the way and not interfere with conversations of business or entertainers and on this night I was standing near the security office when Mr. Irby Mandrell, father of Barbara Mandrell, asked me if I had seen Joe Smith. I knew who he was looking for and told him that I thought he went into the security office and I would help locating him. As we entered the security room, the fellows said "hello Jim what are you doing out here tonight?" Irby looked at me and asked, "Don't you work here?" I told him that I worked for the F.B.I., however, came out often to see the shows and I especially wanted to see this show. He asked that I wait until he finished talking to Mr. Smith. He informed me that he was a former policeman in Corpus Cristi, Texas and he totally respected all law enforcement. I told him that my family thought that the Mandrell family was the best country music family in the business and I had hoped that someday I could meet them and tell them. Mr. Mandrell, stated that we could go back to see Barbara at that time. We were able to spend 15-20 minutes with her and she was very gracious and polite just as we had heard.

The family later moved to California for over two years while they performed the world renown "Mandrell Sisters Show". They would try to come back to Nashville during the "Fan Fair week".

In weeks and months of passing and meeting other members of the family, we all became family. They told us that we were going to have to change our name to "Mandrell."

After retirement from the F.B.I. and the Brady's moved to Hendersonville, we realized that Irby and Mary's wedding anniversary was the same week in November as Verna and I. From that time to seventeen years later, the four of us took a trip that week to some designated location such as Mt. Rushmore, Florida, Myrtle Beach, Branson, cruises, and Pidgeon Forge (very often after Louise opened her theater which she operated for eight years.) Louise originated and operated the "Celebrity's Shoot," where celebrities would come and shoot skeet in competition. After she opened her theater in Pidgeon Forge, her sister, Irlene took over the "Shoot"., and located it in other States as well as Tennessee and I was fortunate enough to continue on the board of directors and shoot until their schedules forced them to discontinue.

We stopped our annual trips because of health issues in both families. After Irby's death occurred in 2009. The remainder of the families are still in very close contact. We miss our friend dearly.

Dad Brady

Mom Brady

Jim Lori, Ann Crook, Verna Brady, and Charlie Chase

Activity Director at Hearth Assisted Living in
Hendersonville, TN, at Halloween Party

Verna Brady and friends visit Barbara Mandrell

Louise, Irlene, Jim, & Barbara Mandrell "The Mandrell Sisters TV Show"

Greatest Granddaughters Stevi and Mia

Jim, SAC Cecil Moses and executive asst. Dir. Lee Colwell

Jim and Ms. Bramlett demonstrate the new NCIC machine to the
Memphis King and Queen of the Memphis Cotton Carnival

Steven and Stan (sons) point the American Flag on their bedroom wall

Jim - Verna
Children & Grand Children

Mr. and Mrs.
Rosenbloom - First
couple we meet at Hearth
Assisted Living

Jim, Governor Mike Huckabee,
Kirby Fudge, and Mrs.
Huckabee,
Backstage at Gov. Huckabees'
TV show taping

Jim & Verna on Cruise with Mr & Ms Irby Mandrell

Supervisory Staff of the Memphis FBI Div.

Jim meets Dir. Kelly at Memphis Airport

Jessica and Robbie Crosslin our cherished 2nd Grandchild to be married

Friends having lunch in Private Dining Room with
Brady's at the Hearth Assisted Living

Jim Brady and Director FBI Webster in Memphis

Entertainers and Friends spend eveing at the Brady's
L to R - Eddie Fulton, Gene Ward, Jeanne Pruett, Connie Bingaman,
Fred Bingham, Jim Brady
Seated: Verna Brady, Jeanne Seely, Steve Brady

Jim - Linda Davis, Tina Brady, Reba McIntire, Skeet Shooting

16

Ray Steven's Cabaray

To celebrate my son and daughter in law's hard week at work, we decided to attend the Cabaray.

Ray and the staff were very cordial to us and we had great food and show and the photos shown here: We can't wait to go back and see the best show in Nashville.

17

Larry's Diner

Many years ago, in 1997, Mr. Larry Black started a recording and TV show entitled family reunion and Larry's Diner. He had many different country music artist in attendance telling stories and singing their popular songs. At the diner, he would have one artist and Nadine would tell stories.

I first met Joey and Rory at the Diner as we did other members of the show. Verna and I were in Illinois visiting mutual friends with Joey, Rory and Nadine, when Joey and Rory announced that they were expecting a child. They were sooo happy. That day was also Joey's birthday.

A few days later Joey was diagnosed with cancer. After surgery and treatment she was diagnosed as in remission to which every one was very grateful.

Little Indiana, their pride and joy, has down syndrome and after Joey got home, she went to the Dr. and it was determined cancer had returned. She spent many months in hospitals and lost her battle with cancer in March 2016. She was buried on their farm cemetary.

Rory has done a tremendous job raising Indiana to the extent of building a small school house on the farm property. This photo shows Rory with Indiana and the other children in school.

We miss Joey very much, but are thankful that Rory, Indiana and the family are doing well.

Larry's Diner with guest Daily and Vincent

18

Catching the thieves of Government Property

In 1966, it was determined that there was a shortage of government property at the Memphis Defense Depot on Airways Blvd. in Memphis, Tennessee. The depot disperses supplies to other military bases. To complicate things, the supplies were missing from the warehouse where my wife worked in the offices of that building. She was totally unaware the shortage of supplies because she only handled the paperwork given to her from the workers in the warehouse.

I would ask her questions regarding her job and the employees in the warehouse at different days and times I had received a map of the warehouses and background checks of the warehouse employees Bureau headquarters made arrangements for us to get a tractor trailer truck and send one of our agents to school and obtain a truck driving license.

We had signs painted on the door (TGP Lines) which meant (Theft of Government Property.)

On one occasion our Agent took the truck with an order for supplies to the depot and as they were loading the truck he told the employee that he sure would like to have a forklift like the one they were using. The employee then asked how much he would pay for one like that. The agent told him that he only had $1500.00 with him. The employee told the agent to open the tailgate of the trailer and he would drive the forklift on for him for $1500.00.

It was determined that eight employees were involved in the theft and the investigation expanded over one year and totaled $100,000.00.

My wife was so mad because at the time of the arrest of the employees, she knew it was the FBI taking her co-workers away and she did not know anything about it. That night I explained that I could not discuss cases with her and especially one where she might be associated with I did it for her safety as well.

19

Bureau Van needed at Tent City

During the marches and tent city in the Memphis Div., it became necessary to have the bureau's specially equipted van for surveillance in the Somerville, TN., and Memphis, areas.

It was determined that the only van available was in the Columbia South Carolina Div.

The sac decided that I should fly to Columbia and drive the van back to the Somerville area.

Due to to the secrecy of the van being an FBI vehicle, it was necessary that new bogus drivers lic., and ID's be issued for plane ticket and any other ID for the Columbia FBI office. My TN., lic and FBI ID was placed into the sac confidential safe. My new ID's reflected the name Anthony J. Silcox.

I was issued a gas credit card reflecting a company in Florida and the van had a Florida lic., plate.

The only problem of the trip was when I stopped for gas and the attendant wanted to check the oil etc., under the hood. I did not want anyone checking under the hood because the battery was special and reached from the radiator to the firewall behind the dashboard. The attendant raised the hood before I could stop him and he backed up asking what I did because he had never seen a battery like that one.

I informed him that I worked for an amusement park located in Florida and we used that to test the electric bumper cars.

He responded "Oh" and that was the end of any problem for the two day trip.

20

Martin Luther King Killed in Memphis

Memphis, TN., was under going a sanitary workers strike in April of 1968 and on several occasions Rev., King and thousands of his followers including Jesse Jackson and other dignitaries would appear in Memphis for a big march on Main Street in protest.

On April 4, 1968, at approx. 6 P.M., Rev. King, Jesse Jackson, Ralph Abernathy and others were standing on the second floor balcony of the Loraine Motel when a gun shot was fired from the rear of a bldg., facing Main Street. The bullet struck King on the right side at a downward angle to the spinal cord and lodged into the shoulder. He was transported to the St. Joseph Hospital and pronounced dead at approx. 7 P. M.

Everyone was called back in to work immediately. I arrived to the scene prior to moving the body from the balcony.

A Memphis police officer received information that a white Mercury Mustang was seen leaving from a parking meter near the front of the bldg., from which the shot was fired from the rear. The officer immediately put out the information state wide as he was rushing to the entrance of the the bldg.. where he located something wrapped in newspaper near the entrance door. He immediately realized that it was a gun. He turned the gun over to one of the Memphis FBI agents and the agent and I took the gun to the office and our firearms instructor and a Sgt. from the Shelby County sheriff's office prepared the gun for shipping to the FBI lab for processing it for bullet comparison and for fingerprints.

A description of a man using the name of Eric Starvo Galt was registered at a motel on Lamar Ave., and was driving a white Mustang. An alert was dispatched for Eric Starvo Galt, however, when the two agents who flew the gun to the lab arrived and the technicians checked for fingerprints, they identified a print as being James Earl Ray. A new alert was put out nation wide for James Earl Ray because it was determined that he was an escapee from prison and now a suspect in the murder of Dr. King.

After approx., two months James Earl Ray was apprehended in London Heathrow Airport with assistance from Scotland Yard, using a false Canadian passport by the name of Ramon George Sneyd.

Two Memphis agents were assigned to transport ray back to Tennessee.

Ray plead guilty to Kings murder and was sentenced to 99 years in prison. He tried unsuccessfully to withdraw his plea and get a retrial, however, was unsuccessful. Ray died in prison in 1997 at the age of 70.

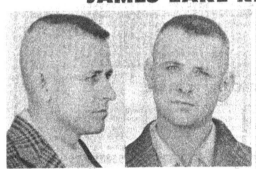

WANTED BY THE FBI

CIVIL RIGHTS – CONSPIRACY
INTERSTATE FLIGHT – ROBBERY
JAMES EARL RAY

FBI No. 405,942 G

Photographs taken 1960

Photograph taken 1968
(eyes drawn by artist)

Aliases: Eric Starvo Galt, W. C. Herron, Harvey Lowmyer, James McBride, James O'Conner, James Walton, James Walyon, John Willard, Jim.

21

"Way to go men!" - my own son

My Son, Steve Brady, a Sargent with the Metro Police Dept in Nashville, TN and his squad confiscated over 500 lbs of marijuana valued at over $700000, which at that time was a record bust. This action originated from an arrest of an individual in possession of six lbs. of marijuana. It was determined through investigation that the 500 lbs came from Mexico through Texas and into Tennessee and to a larger gang arrest which lead to a larger scale Federal Investigation and charges.

The arrest also produced confiscating several firearms including assault rifles with grenade launchers attached.

"WAY TO GO MEN"

22

President Reagan and Press Secretary Jim Brady were shot

I

On March 30, 1981, A friend in Memphis Tennessee pick me up at my home and drove me to the Memphis airport where I had to leave to go to Washington DC. He left me at the airport and then proceeded to take a little girl to school. I arrived in Washington approximately 10 AM and proceeded to the J Edgar Hoover building on Pennsylvania Avenue in Washington. President Reagan, Jim Brady, and a Secret Service agent was shot approximately five blocks from the J. Edgar Hoover Bldg.

- After the subject had been arrested, I telephoned Verna in Memphis and advised her that I was OK because the news media had announced that Jim Brady had been shot and the public sometimes don't distinguish between the F B I and Press Secretary.

Approximately at 2 PM the people who were assigned to go to Quantico Virginia for a week of in-service training at the F B I Academy boarded the bus and left WashingtonD C . When we arrived at Quantico several instructors came to the bus and stated that the authorities in Washington sent Hinkle, the individual who shot President Reagan and Jim Brady to Quantico for safety reasons.

23

"Miburn"

Mississippi Burning Movie

The Civil Rights Movement in the 1960's brought on what was deemed as the Second Reconstruction. There were different organizations started across the country with activities such as sit-ins and in 1961 the Freedom Riders. The Student Nonviolent Coordinating Committee (SNCC), struggled to gain voter rights for African Americans but worked with many organizations to bring awareness to African Americans. The Civil Rights Movement struggled in the 1960's, however, young people were devoted to the movement and continued on through arrests, beatings and even murder.

The Ku Klux Klan did not progress too well after World War II, however, other groups using the structure of the Klan were considered terrorists against African Americans and their communities. The Klan reemerged in 1963 and took hold in Mississippi in 1964 with cross burnings in approximately 65 of the states 82 counties and consequently started an increase in the Klan membership.

The Klan did not hold back on their reign of terror.

Three Civil Rights volunteers, drove to Mississippi after hearing about a Klan attack, but the three workers did not make it very far. They were arrested June 21 by Deputy Price in Neshoba County and were held in jail, while the Klan was waiting and planning to attack. The three were released at nightfall but were stopped within same county by the same Deputy. Each of the men were shot and buried in a dam.

The disappearance of the three workers caused National attention and the FBI, President Johnson, nor Director J. Edgar Hoover could ignore it. The FBI sent hundreds of agents, from several Divisions to investigate the case, code name "MILBURN" (Mississippi Burning). The main focus of the FBI was to find the three workers. On August 4th the corpses were discovered buried under the dam and it was determined how they were murdered.

There were nineteen suspects indicted by the U. S. Justice Department for violating the Workers Civil Rights Act. Seven of the defendants received 3 to 10 yrs., sentence and nine (9) were acquitted. The Jury was deadlocked on three (3) of the subjects.

The case was held in Mississippi but the court delayed the procedures and the murderers did not enter federal prison until 1970.

"Miburn"
(codename for Mississippi Burning)

24

The disappearance of Jimmy Hoffa, Leader of truckers union

The disappearance of Hoffa set off investigations throughout the Bureau and especially in Nashville the states capital and one of the cities Hoffa was last physically seen in 1975.

The SAC sent five cars with agents to cover any leads to locate Hoffa.

The carivan of bucars had to travel State Highway 100 to Nashville because I-40 was not complete at that time.

All agents had to stay in Nashville three days to exhaust all leads.. Many leads were developed to assisted in the attempt to locate Mr. Hoffa, however he was not located in the Nashville, TN., area after his disappearance was discovered.

25

My personal barber becomes 10 Most Wanted

It was routine that each employee would check his/her mail slot for incoming mail each morning and for new instructions and etc.

I pulled out the wanted flyer no. 202 of Henry Clay Overton, whom I personally knew as being my barber in Washington for approximately 2 years. During many conversations, Overton told me about his family, where he lived, about a daughter who lived in Houston, Texas and when he went to see her, he would always travel through Memphis.

I immediately took the flyer to the SAC and told him my story. He called the Bureau and they instructed for him not to let me be on the street alone because Overton was armed and already charges with UFAP (murder).

Three or four days passed and the Virginia Highway Patrol were chasing Overton and traveling over 100 miles per hour on a two lane highway and as he went over a hill, he lost control and hit a man with his wife head on killing all three.

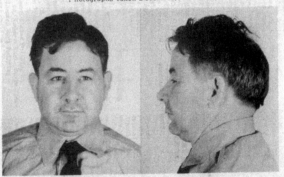

26

Tennessee Governor Ray Blanton sent to Jail

Gov. Leonard Ray Blanton and members of his administration. In 1980, Blanton and two of his aides were indicted for their roles in a scheme to provide liquor license to those who agreed to pay a portion of their profits from the license. Another serious investigation involving Blanton and his cronies was TENNPAR, short for (Tennessee pardon), which investigated the large scale illegal release of serious offenders from the state penitentiary by this state parole board in exchange for bribes. Blanton was convicted and sent to prison. Details of this investigation may be found in the book "FBI codename Tennpar", by Hank Hillin, who led the investigation and wrote the book. During the 1980s Memphis ran an operation "Rocky Top" with the Tennessee Bureau of investigation and the IRS. This joint effort found illegalities and bribery among the charities bingo operators, lobbyists, regulators, and state legislators. State Congressman Randy McNally and House Speaker and later Gov. Ned McWhirter helped the Bureau in the case and received praise for their support. By the end of the operation more than 50 individuals including state legislators were convicted. In one 1980 case work by the FBI and Memphis Police Department, the division investigated two partners who operated a fictitious chop shop targeting commercialized although stripping. The case also led to the recovery of 265 vehicles valued at over $3.6 million, stolen parts worth more than $100,000, 1300 pounds of stolen dynamite, and 166 pounds of marijuana and automatic and other weapons.

27

Billy Dean Anderson: "10 Most Wanted" Killed

June, 1979, many priority cases were being worked in the Memphis Div., of the FBI. One of the most notorious criminals who had been on the FBI's top ten list for approximately five years was Billy Dean Anderson.

Anderson had been convicted of robbery, carrying a concealed weapon, and assault with intent to commit murder. He was an escapee from a Tennessee jail having been convicted of shooting at investigating law enforcement personnel on at least three occasions.

Upon many surveillance attempts and contacts with relatives all with negative results, it was determined by supervisory case agent Cecil Moses that possibly Anderson would appear at his parents residence on her birthday since he was always very close to his mother. It was then determined by Supervisor Moses to set up a permanent surveillance for several days prior and several days after his mothers birthday.. The next decision was how to accomplish this procedure.

Office mgr. Jim Brady had a class A motor home and after discussions of where to park it so that the Anderson home could be observed with telescopes and night glasses, the Bureau decided that they would pay for installing telephones and communication system into the motor home. (In 1979 cell phones were not existing)

The night of capture and Anderson's mother's birthday, agents were dispensed along side of a country road leading to the pasture area behind the Anderson home. Agents crawled to areas in the pasture in order to completely cover the area behind the house.

Subject Anderson and his mother appeared at the back door of the home and said their good-bye's.

Anderson started across the pasture toward one agent and stopped as if he sensed something wrong and turned toward another agent, walking very slowly in the dark. (moon light only)

Upon walking within approx. 15 ft., the agent rose announcing "FBI freeze Billy" at which time Anderson was pullin the slinged rifle from his shoulder to shoot the agent.

The agent shot Anderson and ended a long five year top ten hunt.

WANTED BY THE FBI

INTERSTATE FLIGHT - ASSAULT TO MURDER, ATTEMPTED BURGLARY

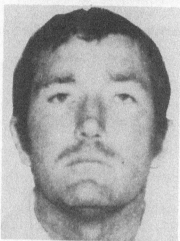

BILLY DEAN ANDERSON

DESCRIPTION

Born July 12, 1934, Fentress County, Tennessee; Height, 5'8''; Weight, 160 to 170 pounds; Build, stocky; Hair, brown; Eyes, blue or green; Complexion, fair; Race, white; Nationality, American; Occupations, artist, mechanic, laborer, tree surgeon, farmer; Scars and Marks, scar across nose, scar left side of forehead, surgical scar right side of stomach, surgical scar lower spine; Remarks, reportedly wears braces on both legs and suffers from atrophy of legs; Social Security Number used, 314–36–7484.

CRIMINAL RECORD

Anderson has been convicted of robbery, carrying a concealed weapon and assault with intent to commit murder.

CAUTION

ANDERSON, WHO IS BEING SOUGHT AS AN ESCAPEE FROM A TENNESSEE JAIL, HAS BEEN CONVICTED OF ASSAULT TO MURDER LAW ENFORCEMENT OFFICERS. ON AT LEAST THREE OCCASIONS HIS SHOOTING AT INVESTIGATING LAW ENFORCEMENT PERSONNEL INCLUDED FIRING AT POINT-BLANK RANGE WHILE EXITING STOPPED VEHICLE AND WITH RIFLE FROM AMBUSH. CONSIDER ARMED, EXTREMELY DANGEROUS AND AN ESCAPE RISK.

FBI/DOJ

28

Lasting Memories — The Freedom Train

On Dec 31, 1986, I retired from the FBI and shortly received a call from my friend, Mr. Henry Harrison, President and Owner of the Rockabilly Museum in Jackson, TN requesting that I meet with him regarding a project he is working.

The project was a Freedom Train leaving Memphis, Tennessee to the final destination of Washington, DC in honor of all veterans of all wars. Mr. Harrison requested that he would like for me to handle the security on the train for the approximately three week tour. When and how the plans for the train to leave Memphis, have the time of arrival in different cities, was working out and I decided that I could and would enjoy doing that for him.

Mr. Harrison had already received commitments from Gen. William Westmoreland, Capt. Eugene McDanial, Tom Moore, and after Johnny Cash heard about it, he wanted to be on the train for the entire trip as it stops in all major cities and a different entertainer would board the train and do a show and a grand Finale was planned in Washington. We had many meetings in Memphis, in the

Elvis suite of the Holiday Inn, and I would go to the airport and pick up Johnny and his manager and take them back to the airport after our meeting.

I had contacted each city's Police, Security Departments and Homeland Security in Washington and we were proceeding with plans. Sadly to say, something happened with the railroad agreements or plans and the trip was cancelled.

SAC Secretary Norworth taking dictation - (1961)
(retired after 60 years)

29

Bingo — Secretary of State commits suicide

Upon retirement from the Bureau, the Brady's moved to Hendersonville, TN., and after building a home I was offered a job with the Tennessee State Charitable and Solicitation Div., of the Secretary of State's Office. The job consisted of inspecting bingo games throughout the state to see that they were within compliance of state laws in operation. I was informed by the FBI that a federal case was being persued and we worked together on this operation until the state supreme court ruled that bingo was a lottery which was against state laws and all games in the state of Tennessee had to stop. At the time of this ruling, there were only 200 bingo games left in the state. Fifty percent of the income was suppose to go to a charity. It was determined that only approximately twenty per cent was accounted for charity.

There were three representatives and senators who were involved in this case convicted and sentenced.

The Secretary of State (who hired me) came out on his back porch and committed suicide. It is believed that he hired me because the Governor was pressing him to get the bingo problems solved in Tennessee.

The next assignment was to the Governors task force for marijuana eradication which lasted from June to October of each year. Most of the time was spent in East Tennessee because more marijuana was raised in the mountains because it was more difficult to spot from the air. We had approximately nine helicopters throughout the state with different crews locating and eradicating the plants.

On one occasion in East Tennessee we brought the chopper down to refuel and to eat lunch. There was a small country store across the street from the schoolyard where we landed and since it was summer, school was out. There was a crowd of people around the local store and a little 10-year-old boy came over across the highway and asked if we were looking for marijuana. He stated that people over at the store I were talking about us looking for marijuana. I asked him if he knew what marijuana looks like and he said that he did not. I told him to come back to one of our trucks and I would show him what marijuana look like. I told him that if he saw this type plant or saw anyone smoking marijuana, to immediately go home and get away from it and tell his mom and dad to call the sheriff and for him to stay away from this type stuff. He said he definitely would. I asked him if he had seen anyone anytime smoking anything that looked like this and he said that he had not he said that his mom smoked but she smoked Prince Albert. I asked him if she smoked a pipe and if he meant that she smoked a pipe with Prince Albert. He told me that she smoked a holder with Prince Albert and she had

TWO TUB FULLS OF PRINCE ALBERT IN THEIR KITCHEN. I asked him where he lived and he pointed up the highway on the left. I told him to go back to the store and the remember what I told him about staying away from marijuana. A group of us were eating lunch and I told them that after we finished we had a chore today and that we needed to get a warrant for the house up the road. Everyone asked why and I told them the story which they could hardly believe. From that day on they joked with me about interrogating a 10-year-old until he told about his mother smoking Prince Albert. During the search of the premises we found marijuana growing behind the barn and charged the man and his wife with growing and possession of controlled substances.

After one year I was assigned to raids of establishments suspected of selling dope where alcohol was sold and also inspecting establishments which had applied for license to sell liquor.

I was also appointed as the representative of ABC to meet with the governors emergency management group from each TN., state agency to plan for state wide emergencies such as earth quakes, floods, bomb threats etc., throughout the state.

After ten years of service in 1997, I retired and started my private investigative agency entitled "Investigative Services & Technologies Inc." This business is still active performing background and pre-screening checks for businesses, colleges, real estate offices and other private investigators.

I was accepted by Omnisec, a division of the United

States Defense Dept., as an investigator on contract, for which I performed these duties for three years. I was forced to discontinue because of family health problems. I am able to continue my background business because I can perform these duties from my home office.

I have performed some type of law enforcement for 65 years as of 2017.

I am tired and
Now
Retiring

_____Please_____

Enjoy the book!!!

30

Snake Territory

AFTER THE GOVERNORS TASK FORCE finished the summer months of assignments, we were back in the Nashville area and had a warrant to search a house in south Nashville. When we arrived and found no one at home, it was necessary to break into the home through the front door. I was one of the first to walk in and as I looked around the room very quickly, and noticed a large python snake lying along the baseboard of the living room. I looked along the baseboard of the right side of the room and noticed another python snake which was even longer. I stated to the other agents that they could have this house however, one of the agents said that he could handle both of them which he did. He stated that he was not afraid of the snakes and he would take care of them. He called the Nashville zoo keeper and they delivered two large cages and the agent placed the snakes into the cages. We did finish searching the house in a very cautious way. No other snakes were were found. A large amount of dope was located in the attached garage. The snakes measured approximately 11 and 13 feet in length.

31

Scam in Phoenix

In 2017, I received a complaint from an individual in Memphis who thought that he was being scammed by an individual in Seattle Washington. He advised that this individual offered him a website from Amazon and that he would receive a percentage on all items sold on this website and it would have his confidential number and he would be paid monthly. He stated there would be 1/2 million items in his website and anyone ordering from that group, is where he would earn his money.

It would cost the complainant in Memphis, a total of $5000 for this website and hook up with Amazon.

He stated that he had observed his website and believed the man to be honest. He had communicated with him on several occasions and he trusted that it was legitimate, however for the last week or two at this point he had been unable to talk to the man. He stated that the phone number was working however no one would answer the phone. He did obtain the man's name, address, phone number, before sending him the $5000.

I started trying to get an answer from the phone number furnished and also did not receive a response.

After checking to see who the phone number was listed to, I realize that this was a scam because it was a fictitious company listed to the number. The next step was to do a background check on the name and get information regarding the individual's family. I found the name with the spouse's name and date of birth near the same, in Phoenix Arizona. I contacted this individual and verified that his information was true and that he was a permanent resident of Arizona for over 20 years with the same spouse and the same employment over 20 years. I asked him if he had done any business with a company in Seattle Washington. His reply was that he had an insurance policy with a company in Seattle, however had been notified that his records had been stolen. After verifying that these records were stolen from this company, I realized that we were looking for a fictitious name and other information so we had to start all over.

I recontacted the complainant in Memphis and asked him how he paid the $5000 to the individual. He stated that he sent it through PayPal. I contacted PayPal and asked them how the receipt for the payment was signed. The clerk at PayPal did not want to furnish that information, however after talking to the supervisor and explaining that it would save them time and money because if I couldn't get the information I would have to subpoena the records, he then agreed to tell me the individuals' name who signed for the money. Now with a new name to look for, I had to start all over trying to locate the individual. I located him in Arizona and through the corporation of the police department in that city found that this individual had been in motorcycle car accident and taken to a hospital in Phoenix Arizona. I contacted four hospitals and located the subject in intensive care in one of the hospital. I immediately notified the FBI Office in Nashville Tennessee because it was a major case of fraud by wire. They said they would notify the FBI Phoenix and proceed with opening case. I contacted the Sgt. at the police department in Arizona of my findings and thanked him for his Cooperation. I asked the supervisor nurse to notify the Phoenix FBI office when this individual was going to be moved from the intensive care to a private. I also checked daily with the nurse regarding his location in intensive care and Friday of that week they told me that the individual had been dismissed.

I contacted the Police Department in the city where this individual lived and in discussion about the case the Sgt. advised me that he remembered an individual in a wreck about a week prior and believed that the individual on the motorcycle was using that name. He stated that he would check and call me back which he did. He stated that the individual was taken to a hospital in Phoenix and in checking those hospitals, located an individual by that name in the intensive care in one of the hospitals. I asked the supervisor nurse to notify the Phoenix FBI Office when this individual was going to be moved from intensive care to a private room. I checked with the nurse daily regarding his location in intensive care and on Friday of that week they told me that the individual had been dismissed. I asked the supervisor if they had notified the FBI and they did not. I notified the Sgt. at the police department, who stated that he remembered that week that the individual had passed away. He checked with others in the department and they all verified the same information. I then called the Board of Funeral Directors who verified that this individual did die and was buried. I notified the Police and the FBI office.

I notified my friend at the FBI and he jokingly said "why don't you come back to work, because you have already opened and closed a case before the Phoenix Office got the case opened."

"I SAID THANKS, BUT I AM TOO OLD TO CUT THE MUSTARD".

"I have tremendous respect and admiration for law enforcement, and I'm very proud that my Daddy was a policeman when I was a young girl. "Many years ago, when Daddy introduced me to Jim Brady, and told me that he was an FBI agent, I was in awe of Jim. Through the years, Jim and Daddy became like brothers to each other. When I could get Jim to tell me stories about some of his time in the FBI, I could understand why I hold him and the FBI in such esteem. I really enjoyed this book of insightful, behind the scenes stories."

–Barbara Mandrell

"This is a compelling recollection of Jim Brady's life, growing up in rural Mississippi; and his outstanding career with the FBI."
"To know, and to have worked with him, is to *love* him.
"I highly recommend this book to you."

–*Cecil E. Moses,* Retired, Special Agent and Charter Member of the FBI's Senior Executive Service

"Jim Brady served as a senior administrative FBI employee for over 30 years. He earned the respect of FBI officials as well as subordinates and FBI employees in other field offices. He was a model administrator."

–*Dr. Lee Colwell,* Associate Director, FBI, Retired

Writing a few lines for Jim Brady's book is a pleasure, not a task. You see, Jim is one of my top five best and closest friends; and one of the finest and best persons I've ever known, a devout Christian Southern Gentleman. I have know Jim since 1962, when he met my plane at the Memphis Airport; then drove me and two other FBI agents directly to Oxford, Mississippi, to join a group of FBI employees assembled there to represent the Bureau's interest in a riot about to take place on the campus at the University of Mississippi, (Ole Miss).

Our boss in that operation was Special Agent in-charge Karl Dissly, whose philosophy of leadership was, as he told me: assign the best people you have to do the job, and then get out of the way.

SAC Dissly had done that with Jim Brady, keeping us all straight and on task ... that week of firearms being discharged, cars being burned, screaming and yelling student agitators breaking windows; all rioting.

Well, I saw the best at work that weekend in Jim Brady, and he's been my friend and fellow FBI employee since. Jim Brady has served a number of FBI bosses in every kind of case since then and he shows the same kind of care and concern in this book.

–*Hank Hillin*, FBI Agent, 1955-1980; 1981 Elected Sheriff, Nashville, Tennessee, Past Army Intelligence Agent